Nelson Mandela

Nelson and Winnie Mandela

JUNIOR ■ WORLD ■ BIOGRAPHIES

Nelson Mandela

BRIAN FEINBERG

CHELSEA JUNIORS
a division of CHELSEA HOUSE PUBLISHERS

Chelsea House Publishers
EDITOR-IN-CHIEF: Remmel Nunn
MANAGING EDITOR: Karyn Gullen Browne
COPY CHIEF: Juliann Barbato
PICTURE EDITOR: Adrian G. Allen
ART DIRECTOR: Maria Epes
DEPUTY COPY CHIEF: Mark Rifkin
ASSISTANT ART DIRECTOR: Noreen Romano
MANUFACTURING MANAGER: Gerald Levine
SYSTEMS MANAGER: Lindsey Ottman
PRODUCTION MANAGER: Joseph Romano
PRODUCTION COORDINATOR: Marie Claire Cebrián

JUNIOR WORLD BIOGRAPHIES

EDITOR: Remmel Nunn

Staff for NELSON MANDELA
COPY EDITOR: Laurie Kahn
PICTURE RESEARCHERS: Linda Peer, Jonathan Shapiro
SENIOR DESIGNER: Marjorie Zaum
COVER ILLUSTRATOR: Eileen McKeatney

First Printing

1 3 5 7 9 8 6 4 2

Library of Congress Cataloging-in-Publication Data
Feinberg, Brian.
    Nelson Mandela/Brian Feinberg.
      p. cm.—(Junior world biographies)
    Summary: A biography of the black South African leader, focusing on his
struggle to overthrow the tyrannies of apartheid.
    ISBN 0-7910-1569-6
    1. Mandela, Nelson, 1918–   —Juvenile literature.
2. Civil rights workers—South Africa—Biography—Juvenile literature.
3. African National Congress—Biography—Juvenile literature. 4. Political
prisoners—South Africa—Biography—Juvenile literature. [1. Mandela,
Nelson, 1918–   . 2. Civil rights workers. 3. Blacks—
Biography. 4. South Africa—Race relations.]
I. Title. II. Series.
DT1949.M35F45 1992
324.268′083′092—dc20   90-20974
[B]   CIP
[92]   AC

Contents

Zulus and other African tribes ruled South Africa before white settlers captured the land.

1

The People Who Were Not Free

Everyone is special in some way. No two people have the same thoughts and feelings, and just about no one looks exactly like anyone else. Some people have brown hair, some are blond, and others are redheaded. There are many different skin colors, too, and people are often given labels because of that. Those with light skin are called white, even though they are not really the color of a sheet of paper. People with darker skin are often called black, although in the United States, many blacks prefer to be called African Americans, because hundreds of years ago their families were taken from Africa to be sold as slaves.

No matter how different one person may look from another, however, the laws of the United States were designed to provide everyone with the same rights and opportunities. But the American laws are not perfect, and black Americans, especially, have often been denied their legal rights.

In America, there has been some improvement in the way that peoples of different races relate to each other. In Africa, however, there is a nation where differences in skin color are still the cause of terrible problems. Africa itself is a huge body of land called a continent, and it contains many different countries. One of these countries, on the southern tip of the continent, is called South Africa. For many years, the laws there have prevented people with dark skin from having the same rights as white people have. Black South Africans have been forced to live only in certain areas. Until a few years ago, they had to carry special passes to travel through and work in the cities where whites live. They have never been allowed the right to help choose their nation's leaders.

It is not easy to understand why this happened. Sometimes one group of people tries to grab the most privilege and power for itself because it believes that it is better than all others. Sometimes people fear that they will lose something if everyone is given the same rights and privileges they have.

No matter what reasons the South African government may have for denying blacks equal rights, the black people of that country are angry because they have not been treated fairly. They know that they are equal to whites and deserve to have the same rights as white South Africans. They also know that they were there first, because their ancestors lived on the African continent many years before the whites arrived. There are about 28 million blacks in South Africa, compared to 5 million whites. Black South Africans argue that there are more than enough resources there for both blacks and whites because the country they share is large and bountiful.

South Africa has rolling hills, towering mountains, and deep valleys. Some parts of the country are hot and wet, but others are dry desert. The plants that grow there also vary greatly from one place to another. Some areas have short grasses and shrubs, and others have thick forests. A lot of the forest has disappeared, however, because people have moved into the countryside and cleared it away. Lions, giraffes, zebras, and monkeys may still be seen, but like the forests, many of the animals have disappeared because their habitats have been destroyed.

Compared to most other African nations, South Africa is highly developed. Most of the country's wealth comes from minerals mined from the ground. South Africa is especially rich in gold, copper, uranium, and coal. These minerals, as well as the crops from South Africa's fertile farmland, have created an economy rich enough to create large cities such as Cape Town, Johannesburg, and Pretoria.

It is not wealth, however, that truly separates South Africa from the other nations of the continent. South Africa has a unique political system and an especially bloody history. The people who rule South Africa today are white. They have been in the country since 1652, when their Dutch

Black South Africans have been given fewer rights than have the white people of their country, and many of the blacks have been forced to live in poverty.

ancestors, the Afrikaners, first arrived. The Afrikaners took control of the land, put many blacks into slavery, and treated all blacks as inferiors. Then, in 1806, the British attacked the Afrikaners and took over their settlements. In the years that followed, the British gave blacks more rights and freed the slaves. In response, most Afrikaners moved farther into the interior of South Africa. Battling Zulus and other African tribes, they captured more land for themselves, and once again white settlers ruled black Africans and took away their rights.

In 1899, the Dutch and British fought over this new land. The war lasted three years, and once more the British won. Even though the British now controlled all of the Dutch land, however, the black people won no new rights. In fact, they soon lost some of the ones they already had: In 1913, a law was passed that forced black South Africans out of their homes and placed them in special territories.

Even though the blacks far outnumbered the whites, they were now given a much smaller amount of land. This made it much harder for black people to own farms and earn a living. To make money, many of them had to work for the whites, who paid them very little. The white South Africans also created a new law that required black men to carry a special pass when they were traveling through the territories reserved for whites. Black men could not go into a white city unless they were working there, and they often could not bring their families. When their work was done, they had to go back home.

Today South Africa is an independent nation, but it is still ruled by whites. This book tells the story of a black man who has been fighting all of his life to change that.

Nelson Mandela was once a fine amateur boxer, but his biggest fight has been the battle for equal rights.

CHAPTER

2

The Man Who
Wanted
Freedom

On July 18, 1918, Nelson Mandela was born in a small South African village. In addition to his English name, he was also given a long African name that means "stirring up trouble." His family was a very important part of the Thembu tribe. Nelson's great-great-grandfather had been a respected African king, and his father was an adviser to the most powerful chief of the tribe.

As a boy, Nelson grew up happy and carefree, plowing the village fields and tending cattle and sheep. His first school was a simple building with a thatched roof, but later he went to a Methodist school. In the evenings, Nelson would sit by the fire and listen to the old men of the tribe talk of the days long before the white men came, when the black people of South Africa ruled themselves.

By the time Nelson was 12 years old, his father could already tell that his son had the makings of a leader. But Nelson's father was very sick, and knew that he would not live long enough to see his son grow into a man. He asked the Thembu chief to raise Nelson, and the chief agreed. After his father died, Nelson went to live in the grand palace.

One of the chief's duties was to be the tribe's judge, responsible for settling legal arguments between his people. When two tribespeople had a disagreement, they would gather before the chief, who would hold a trial. Nelson found this so exciting that he decided to become a lawyer. With this goal in mind, Nelson left home for college.

By now he was a strong, handsome man who stood six feet tall. He was a good boxer and a fine student. Away from his village, however, Nelson came face-to-face with the way blacks were treated by the whites who ruled South Africa. At his college, black students had a lot of say in how their school was run. But while he was there, the white authorities decided to take much of that power away. Nelson tried to stop this by organizing a *protest*. A protest happens when a group of people get together to fight against something they believe is unfair. In this case, Nelson helped convince his fellow students not to go to class until the school agreed to give them back the rights they had lost. Instead of winning back the students' rights, however, Nelson was suspended from school and had to return home.

Back in the village, the chief wanted Nelson to give up his protest and return to college, but Nelson refused. He also discovered that the chief had chosen a wife for him, instead of letting

Nelson find one for himself. It was the Thembu tribe's custom to choose wives for its men, but Nelson did not want to marry the woman the chief had picked. Instead, he ran away from the tribe and moved to the city of Johannesburg. Here, he had greater freedom to choose his own path in life.

His first job was as a security guard at a gold mine, but it was not long before the Thembu chief found out where he was working. Nelson decided to leave his job rather than face the chief again. A friend lent him enough money to finish college, and Nelson later went to law school.

Nelson worked for a law firm while attending school. There was a secretary at the firm who worked for the white lawyers, but when she had extra time she would often ask Nelson if he had any work for her. One day Nelson was giving her something to do when one of the firm's white clients came in. The secretary was embarrassed because she did not want the client to think that a black man was her boss. She quickly took some money from her purse, gave it to Nelson, and told him to run to the drug store to get her some shampoo.

Things like this happened all over South Africa. The Afrikaners tried to make black people feel less important than white people. The government had rules to keep blacks and whites as separate from each other as possible. This system was called *apartheid*, an Afrikaner word meaning "apartness." Under apartheid, blacks were not allowed to live in many areas, and there were separate bathrooms, park benches, and even entrance doors set aside for whites only.

These were the kinds of things that Nelson wanted to change. While still a young man, he joined a group of black South Africans who had been seeking equal rights for many years. This group was called the African National Congress, or ANC, and Nelson Mandela has remained a member to this day.

Almost 30 years ago, protestors waited outside a court building in the city of Pretoria. Inside, Nelson Mandela was sentenced to life in prison.

3

The Fight
for Freedom

In 1949, Mandela and the African National Congress decided that it would be best to find peaceful ways to convince the government to give black people equal rights. By joining with other groups that were interested in the same goals, the ANC became stronger than it would have been alone. Together, these groups led a protest that they hoped would make their point. On June 26 of the following year, blacks throughout South Africa were asked to stay home from work. This type of protest is called a *strike*, and because black workers did much of the country's labor, this strike was bound to make the government very angry. The strike was a dramatic success. In Johannesburg, for example, almost three quarters of the black workers stayed home, and protesters demonstrated throughout the country.

But Nelson Mandela did not stop there. Night after night he visited the towns where his people lived, to spread the word that it was time for black South Africans to stand up for their freedom. Nelson also told them that these protests had to be peaceful. There would be no fists, knives, or guns.

There were more protests as the weeks passed. Blacks throughout the nation began to stand up against the way they were treated and the way they were forced to live. But they paid a high price for their actions. One night, Nelson and many other protestors were arrested and put in jail. A guard pushed one of the protestors down some steps, and the man broke his ankle. When Mandela complained, the guard beat him with a nightstick. Despite the beating, Mandela demanded that the protestor be allowed to see a doctor, but the injured man had to wait until morning to have his ankle treated, and spent all night suffering.

As protests spread throughout the country, more and more black South Africans were arrested. The government refused to change its unjust laws and now aimed some of them at Mandela himself. For a time, the government made it a crime for Mandela to travel anywhere beyond Johannesburg.

With the authorities of South Africa working so hard against them, Mandela and the African National Congress found it harder than ever to lead their people. The government was also doing its best to put Mandela back in jail, where he could organize no more protests.

Nelson's life had become very difficult, even dangerous, but some wonderful things happened too. In 1957, a friend introduced Nelson to a young woman named Winnie Madikizela. She was attractive and college educated, a woman with a strong spirit and an independent mind. Her father and mother had both been teachers, and

Winnie was a social worker. But Nelson was older than Winnie, and she was shy around the man who had become so famous among their people. Even so, the two of them fell in love, and it was not long before they were married and moved into a small brick house near Johannesburg.

Winnie knew, though, that their life together would not be an easy one. Nelson had been married once before, but the many problems he faced in his struggle for black freedom had been too difficult for his first wife to bear. She and

Black South Africans have been fighting unfair laws that separate them from whites. This man, for example, is ignoring a sign on the bench that says Europeans [whites] Only.

Nelson had been divorced a year earlier. Now Winnie was going to share Nelson's life, but not even she could know how truly difficult that would be.

Winnie's troubles started early in their marriage. New laws had been passed that required black women to have special permission to travel to certain parts of the country. Of course, there already were laws in place that forced black men to carry special travel passes, but until this time, women had been allowed to move freely from place to place. Winnie took part in a protest against these new laws, even though she was pregnant at the time. She and more than a thousand other women were arrested and put in prison. She was jostled and shoved during the arrest and almost lost her baby before it was born. It was two weeks before she was set free.

Meanwhile, widespread protests against the cruel laws of South Africa continued, and the government made several bloody attempts to stop them. During one protest, police shot at thousands of unarmed blacks, killing 67 of them. That same evening, during another protest, 14 more black people were killed.

Still, black South Africans would not give up. Nelson and other black leaders asked their people to go on strike for two days, starting May 29, 1961. When the government learned of this, it tried to frighten blacks away from the protest. More than 10,000 blacks were arrested even before the strike began. The government patrolled black neighborhoods in armored cars and flew above them in helicopters. In the end, many blacks were too afraid to go on strike, and the second day of the protest had to be canceled.

Finally, Nelson and many other members of the African National Congress had had enough of the government's threats, beatings, and killings. Because peaceful protest had not worked, the ANC decided to become freedom fighters: If the government was going to use violence to try to stop blacks from gaining their freedom, then black South Africans would use violence to make the government think differently. This decision changed the course of Nelson Mandela's life.

Nelson Mandela and Winnie Madikizela were married in 1958.

Black protestors now started to use weapons to blow up electrical power stations, railroads, and government offices. The freedom fighters did what they could to make sure that no one was killed in these attacks, because the ANC had decided that only buildings and machinery should be destroyed.

The government knew that Nelson was involved in these bombings and tried to place him under arrest. This time, however, he stayed hidden and wore different disguises to fool the authorities. One day he might pretend to be a window washer, and another day he might disguise himself as a policeman.

Once, when Nelson was disguised as a chauffeur, a black policeman recognized him. As the policeman walked up to him, Mandela feared that he was about to be arrested. Instead, the policeman winked at him, gave him a special ANC salute, and walked away.

While he was in hiding, Nelson left South Africa to visit other nations, where he sought help for the freedom fighters. Unfortunately, this meant that he had little time to spend with his family. But as he once said, "The struggle is my life." He had promised to fight for freedom until the end of his days.

When Nelson returned to South Africa he continued to work for black equality, but not even he could escape the government forever. On August 5, 1962, Nelson was captured by the South African police while he was once again disguised as a chauffeur. He was put on trial later that year. The government could not prove that he was connected with the protest bombings, but the authorities accused him of organizing one of the large strikes and of leaving the country without permission.

Nelson knew that he could not get a fair trial. He told the court that he had done no wrong, even though he had broken the laws of South Africa. It was clear that he felt the same way the Founding Fathers of the United States had, more than 200 years before. They had to break the laws of England to become free in 1776. Now Nelson Mandela believed that the black people of South Africa had to break the laws of their nation to win their own freedom. "If I had my time over," he said, "I would do the same again. So would any man who dares call himself a man."

The judge found Nelson guilty of both charges and sentenced him to five years at hard labor. Just before he was taken away, he told the court that he was not afraid to go to prison. "Not I alone but all of us are willing to pay the penalties we may have to pay," he said. Then he shouted *Amandla!* three times to the black audience who had come to watch the trial. The audience re-

In 1962, Nelson Mandela was put on trial, charged with leaving South Africa without permission and with encouraging his people to go on strike. Winnie Mandela attended the trial in traditional African tribal clothing.

sponded by shouting back *Ngawethu!* Together, the words mean "Power to the people!"

Before long Nelson found himself in even greater danger. By now, the government had found enough evidence against him to accuse him of treason. The authorities believed that he and other members of the ANC had been trying to start a war against South Africa to win the blacks' freedom. Nelson was put on trial again. If the court found him guilty this time, he might be sentenced to die.

Instead of hiring a lawyer, Mandela conducted his own defense during the trial. He spoke for more than four hours, explaining why he had changed from a peaceful man to one who believed that violence would make his country better. He told how poverty was hurting his people and said that the needs of black South Africans were the same as those of whites. Nelson was again found guilty, but the judge was impressed by his speech and did not sentence him to hang. Instead, Nelson was told that he would spend the rest of his life in prison.

Imprisoned on Robben Island, Nelson Mandela spent many years at hard labor.

4

The Island
Prison

Nelson and other black freedom fighters were sent to a prison called Robben Island. A flat, rocky place swept by the wind and surrounded by rough sea, Robben Island was to be their home for many years to come. They arrived one winter's day in 1964. At first, the prisoners had only a prison uniform and two blankets to keep them warm during the cold nights. The days were no easier. Nelson and the others got up at five o'clock in the morning, took a cold shower, and ate a taste-less porridge for breakfast. After that, they were chained together and taken to a limestone quarry to break rocks in the misty chill of winter or under the blazing summer sun. Some of the prisoners were beaten brutally by the guards. For a long time, their food was to be little more than the awful porridge and some rotten vegetables.

But Nelson was determined to show the prison authorities that he would not break under their cruel treatment. On the first day that he and the other prisoners were sent out to smash rocks, the guards ordered them to run to the quarry. Instead, Nelson convinced his fellow prisoners to walk as slowly as possible. From the start, Nelson proved that he was still a leader. But he spent 18 years on Robben Island, at least 6 of them breaking rocks.

Life in prison also meant that Nelson again saw very little of his family. He was permitted only one half-hour visit with Winnie every six months, and he was not allowed to see his children until they were teenagers. He could receive only one letter every six months, and he was permitted to send one every six months. But Nelson kept a photo of Winnie next to his bed and kissed it every morning.

On the few occasions when Winnie did visit Nelson, they were not permitted to be alone together. On her trips to Robben Island, Winnie was taken to a dimly lit room to meet him. They were separated by a thick piece of glass, making it impossible for Winnie to see her husband clearly. Nelson and Winnie could talk to and hear each other through the glass only by wearing special telephone earphones, and they had to be very careful about what they said. The prison authorities insisted that the Mandelas talk only about family matters. Otherwise, the earphones would be disconnected and the conversation would have to end. Even so, Winnie and Nelson invented a secret code that let them talk about certain things without the guards catching on.

Back home near Johannesburg, it was almost as if Winnie were in prison herself. Not only was she lonely without her husband, but she could see only a few of her friends. Many of the others were in jail or had escaped from South Africa. For the first six months after Nelson went to prison, the government would not even allow Winnie to travel beyond Johannesburg. The government also allowed only one visitor in her house

South African laws have prevented blacks from sharing many areas with whites. Here a black man is allowed to walk through a park but is forbidden to stop and spend time there.

at a time, to keep her from helping the freedom fighters. When the prison authorities finally let Nelson send her his first letter, Winnie read it again and again, because she knew it would be six months before the next one arrived.

Police shot and killed black protestors in 1976, setting off riots throughout the country.

5

The Blood
of Children

Meanwhile, Winnie struggled to support herself and her and Nelson's two daughters, Zeni and Zindzi. The government made it very hard for Winnie to find work and earn money, because both she and her husband had played a part in the fight for freedom. She was forced to quit her job as a social worker, and each time she found a new job, the police would bully her employer into firing her. Sometimes Winnie was hired on a

Monday morning and fired the same afternoon. To get money she took low-paying jobs and had to accept charity from friends.

As horrible as life had become for Winnie, the government wanted to make her suffer even more. The police were always finding ways to frighten her and the children. They paid un-friendly visits to her home three or four times a day and listened in on her telephone calls. Winnie even found out that some of her friends had really been spies for the police. She was arrested so often that her children never knew if she would be there when they got home from school.

When she was a teenager, Winnie's daughter Zindzi published a poem about these difficult years. She wrote

I need a neighbor who will live a teardrop away.
Who will open up when I knock late at night.
I need a child who will play a smile away.
Who will always whisper I love you to be
my mommy.

Eventually, Winnie sent her daughters to a school outside the country to protect them from the government and police. Winnie also became more and more involved in the fight for freedom. At first she thought of herself as "just a little girl fumbling along," but she became an important member of the struggle. On one occasion, for example, she organized a group of women to write letters to members of the African National Congress who had been thrown into jail.

In 1969, the government accused Winnie of threatening law and order in South Africa. She was thrown into prison without trial and spent the next 17 months there. During that time, Winnie was forced to live in a tiny, filthy cell and given food that was not fit to eat. The light in her cell was kept on all the time, and she could not tell when it was day or night. Winnie was so lonely that once, when she saw two ants in her cell, she played with them for hours. Later she said, "You cannot imagine the joy there was in seeing a living creature."

Not long after Winnie was put in prison, the police began to question her. They wanted to get enough evidence to keep her in jail. They questioned her for five days straight, day and night. The only breaks she had came when she fainted, and when she woke up, the police would begin questioning her again.

Winnie was finally brought to trial not once but twice. Yet the government had no solid evidence to prove that she had committed a crime. She was found innocent of the charges and set free. None of this convinced Winnie to give up the fight for her people, instead, she became even more determined to battle injustice.

Even mysterious attempts on her life did not scare Winnie off. One night, three men broke into her home and tried to strangle her. The men ran away when Winnie's niece, who had been staying there, screamed and woke the neighbors.

Meanwhile, as the years passed and Nelson remained in jail, he found his own ways to fight injustice. He led protests against the cruel way he and the other prisoners were treated. For example, the prisoners would sometimes go on a *hunger strike* and refuse to eat anything until their jailers made some improvement. On other occasions, the prisoners might purposely work very slowly. Eventually, the prisoners began to be treated more like people and less like slaves. Nelson helped them win better food and clothing, more blankets, a prison library, and the right to exercise. In addition, the prisoners no longer had to break rocks and were allowed to receive more letters and visits.

Changes were occurring around the nation too. Young black South Africans were becoming more willing than ever to stand up to unfair treatment. But the government still did not give them equal rights. Instead, the new protests led to the worst fighting yet between blacks and whites, beginning when the government tried to tamper with education.

Not surprisingly, the government had not been providing much support for black schools, which were overcrowded and in poor condition. Rather than improve the black schools, however, the government made what seemed to many to be a pointless change. In 1976 the government required black students to take certain courses in Afrikaner instead of in English. On June 16 of that year, 20,000 schoolchildren protested by marching through the black area called Soweto. The police released dogs against the children. When that did not stop the students, the police began shooting. Some of the students were killed, including a 13-year-old boy who was shot from behind.

After that, it was as if the police had set fire to dynamite. Black South Africans exploded with anger over the shootings. For a year, blacks held violent protests throughout the nation. Government offices were destroyed, and protestors fought with police. In the end, about 1,000 protestors were killed and more than 4,000 were wounded. The police arrested about 13,000 blacks.

The government now saw that black citizens would not be frightened away by the army and police. Meanwhile, thousands of blacks had joined the fight for freedom.

Winnie Mandela never stopped fighting for freedom, even after the government banished her to the poor, small village of Brandfort.

6

Mother of
the Country

The South African government thought of a new way to help stop black protests. In 1977, Winnie Mandela was forced to move to a poor, small village far from the people who had joined the struggle for freedom.

The village was called Brandfort, and Winnie's home was a three-room house made of cement blocks. The building had no electricity, running water, or indoor bathroom, and the floors were made of dirt. A police commander told her, "This is the end of the road for you, Winnie Mandela. This time we are going to make you pay in a way you will never forget. From now on, you are going to live in Brandfort till you die." What he did not count on was Winnie's remarkable courage.

The other blacks living in Brandfort were no better off than Winnie. Children were sick because they did not have enough food, and there were no doctors or nurses to take care of them. The authorities had told the other black villagers not to talk to Winnie, but that did not stop her from becoming friends with the people of Brandfort. They grew to respect Winnie because she stood up for herself.

One day, for example, she had to make a telephone call, so Winnie stood in line to use the only public phone in town, even though it was supposed to be for whites only. White people began shouting insults at her, but they did not frighten her away. In fact, Winnie stayed on the phone longer than she needed to, just to show that she could not be scared off. After that, she walked into the whites-only grocery store to do some shopping, and the owner was too amazed to try to stop her. Other black Africans in the village began to follow her example by shopping in stores meant for whites only and by using the public telephone.

Winnie did many other things for the community too. She arranged to get medical supplies, so that a health clinic could open up, and she bought a used car to bring medical care to farms located far from the village. Winnie also set up a soup kitchen and bakery to ease Brandfort's hunger problem. She even turned the empty field around her house into a real lawn, with grass, fruit trees, shrubs, flowers, and a vegetable garden. Winnie had her family with her as well. Her daughter Zindzi would stay in Brandfort when she was home from school. Her other daughter,

Zeni, had married a prince from another African country called Swaziland and had children. It is an African custom for grandmothers to raise children until they are ready for kindergarten, so Winnie also had three grandchildren around the house.

Her strength and courage during those years in Brandfort won Winnie a special name from black South Africans. They called her Mother of the Country. Her fame also spread to other nations. Important people from around the world flocked to the poor little village to meet her. When a reporter asked Winnie whether the hardships she faced had ever made her give up hope, she replied, "Of course not. How can I lose hope when I know that in truth this country is ours and that we'll get it back!" The many troubles in her life, she explained, were necessary to gain the freedom her people deserved.

Nelson Mandela was also achieving greater and greater fame, even though he was still a prisoner on Robben Island. People around the world heard about the man condemned to prison because he had fought for freedom. In fact, it seemed that the longer Nelson was in prison, the more famous he became.

In the meantime, Nelson helped to educate and train young prisoners on Robben Island to continue the fight for freedom when they were released. The government decided to put a stop to this by moving Nelson and other freedom fighters to another jail. They were sent to Pollsmoor Prison, which was just outside the city of Cape Town. In some ways, Pollsmoor was even worse than Robben Island. On Robben Island, each man had been allowed his own cell, and the prisoners had been free to walk about and talk to each other. Here, however, Nelson and the other freedom fighters were forced to live together in one large cell.

A few years after Nelson got to Pollsmoor, however, something changed for the better. For the first time in 20 years, he was allowed to see Winnie without having a glass wall between them. When they met, the two hugged each other for a very long time.

By then, people around the world were demanding that South Africa release Nelson Mandela from prison. At the same time, the African National Congress was again making violent attacks against the government. In one of these attacks, people were killed, including innocent black people. When Nelson heard about this, he said that he was sorry that such a tragedy had occurred. But he still believed that violence was necessary, because the government had not listened to peaceful protests.

In the meantime, changes were taking place in the government, but few of them were for the better. In 1978, a man named P. W. Botha had become the president of South Africa. Like the leaders before him, he wanted to make sure that white people kept all of the power for them-

Winnie Mandela's remarkable courage has inspired children and adults alike.

selves. Other African countries were helping black South Africans in their fight for freedom, and President Botha punished these nations by attacking their railroads and shipping ports.

But Botha also wanted to put a stop to the black protests. He decided to give black South Africans a few new rights without giving them anything close to full equality. He hoped that this would keep the protestors quiet. Botha's changes made it easier for black people to rent houses and to run their own businesses, and blacks were allowed to buy land, though only in areas reserved for them. Black workers were also allowed to take better jobs and the government got rid of the law that prevented people of different races from getting married. In addition, black South Africans no longer needed special traveling passes.

But at the same time, the government forced more blacks than ever to move to parts of the country that had been specially set aside for them, instead of letting them live where they wanted. These areas were the same ones that the government had reserved for blacks at the beginning of the century. Now, however, the government called these areas "homelands," but they were little more than slums. As more and more blacks were forced to live in them, the homelands became terribly overcrowded. People became sick and starved there, and many infants died.

On February 11, 1990, Nelson Mandela was freed from prison. After walking through the prison gates, he raised his arms in a Black Power salute.

7

Sticks Against Tanks

Seeing that the government still was not giving them the freedom they deserved, black South Africans continued to hold protests. In turn, the government used the army and police to try to stop them. Many angry black people began to fight these troops and refused to go to work until the army and police left their towns. They also demanded that the government free Nelson Mandela and other prisoners who had been jailed during the fight for freedom. The protest grew as hundreds of thousands of students joined.

Things soon became even worse. In March 1985, the police killed more than 20 blacks during a funeral, and black South Africans seethed with outrage. Battles between the army and the black protestors became so violent that it seemed as if a civil war had broken out. The protestors believed that violence had become the only way to get the freedom they demanded. The government believed that violence was the only way to stay in control and stop the protests. Neither side would give in.

The fighting also showed the rest of the world how terrible life had become for blacks in South Africa. In the United States, news programs showed footage of young black South African boys using sticks and stones against the army's tanks. TV audiences also saw protestors being beaten and whipped by the police. Americans became angry and many of them wanted to punish the government of South Africa.

Many large corporations in the United States had done business in South Africa for a long time. This had helped the American corporations make money, and it also made a lot of money for white South Africa. But now U.S. citizens began to insist that American companies stop doing business in South Africa. They believed that it was wrong to support a country that was hurting so many people. Many American corporations heeded this call and closed their offices in South Africa.

For the same reason, some big banks in the United States decided to stop lending money to the South African government or its businesses. Companies and banks in many European nations did similar things. People in the United States also began to hold protests against South Africa. The South African government has diplomatic offices in America, including an embassy in Washington. Now thousands and thousands of Americans marched to these offices to show the South African government how angry they were about the way blacks were being treated. In some cases when the protestors were told to leave, they refused and the police arrested them. But for these people, going to jail was not something to be ashamed of; it was something to be proud of, because they were standing up for the rights of others. Black singer Stevie Wonder was one of the people who went to prison. Amy Carter, the daughter of former U.S. president Jimmy Carter, was another protestor who ended up in jail.

Then, on May 1, 1986, more than a million blacks throughout South Africa refused to go to work for one day, as another protest for freedom. Everywhere the government turned, it seemed, South Africa was being punished for its cruel treatment of blacks.

In the meantime, Nelson Mandela's fame, as well as his great dignity and spirit, had won the respect of the very government that was keeping him prisoner. At Pollsmoor Prison he was allowed to tend his own garden, where he grew tomatoes and strawberries. He was also allowed to read newspapers and magazines and to see more visitors.

During his time in prison, Nelson worked hard to stay fit. Even when he was more than 60 years old, he would get up at 3:30 every morning and do 2 hours of exercise. Still, prison life was not healthy for a man of his age. In 1988, he was taken to a hospital to be treated for a serious disease called tuberculosis.

When he was well enough, Nelson was moved to another jail. But this time he was allowed to live in a house on the prison grounds instead of in a cell. Three white guards kept watch over him, and in time Nelson won them over as friends. By now the prison authorities were speaking to him respectfully and calling him Mr. Mandela.

Because Nelson was so famous, the government knew that it could not let him die in prison. That would make South Africa look even worse than it already did to the rest of the world. Now the government began to think of ways to release Mandela from jail and still keep him from leading the fight for freedom.

Nelson was told that he could leave prison, but only if he agreed to certain conditions. The government said that he would have to leave the country, or stay in just one part of South Africa, or promise that he would encourage his people to make only peaceful protests. Nelson said no to each offer. He would leave prison only if there were no strings attached.

The world has seen many changes since the day Nelson Mandela was sent to prison. In Eastern Europe, Communist governments have had to give up their power and let new, democratic governments move in. East Germany and West Germany have reunited to form a single, free nation, when only a short time ago a huge wall divided a Communist government in the east from a democratic government in the west.

Today, even stubborn South Africa has changed somewhat. In 1989, a new president, F. W. de Klerk, took over. Unlike the men who came before him, de Klerk realized that the government must reach a peaceful agreement with black South Africans. To help make this happen, he released some of the people who had been sent to jail during the struggle for freedom. One of the prisoners he freed was Nelson Mandela.

During a visit to New York City, Nelson Mandela gave a speech to thousands of people at Yankee Stadium.

CHAPTER

8

A Free Man

On February 11, 1990, Nelson Mandela became a free man again. The government still had not granted equal rights to black South Africans, but releasing Nelson was a sign that this day would come. When he stepped through the prison gates, hundreds of black people were there to try to catch a glimpse of him and to celebrate his release. Nelson was now 71 years old, thin, and gray haired. He had spent 27 years in prison, but that had not weakened his spirit one bit. Nelson faced the people and raised first one arm and then the other in a Black Power salute.

Nelson's next stop was the city of Cape Town. Tens of thousands of people gathered there to hear him give his first speech since he had been sent to prison so many years earlier. When he spoke, Nelson showed that he had not changed his ideas about his people's fight for freedom. The government would have to prove that it was ready to sit down and talk peacefully with black leaders, he said. Only then would his people give up their violent protests.

Even so, when black South Africans do win their freedom, Nelson does not want to take rights away from white people. He wants everyone to share power. "Whites in South Africa belong here," he once said. "This is their home." Nelson has also said, "Whites are fellow South Africans, and we want them to feel safe." His true wish is for each person in South Africa to have an equal vote in government elections.

Since Nelson Mandela's release, he and Winnie have spent some of their time traveling outside of South Africa, asking other countries to help convince the South African government to change its laws. When he visited England, a pop music concert was held in his honor. More than 70,000 people attended. Nelson gave a speech there that was broadcast to millions of people around the world.

In June 1990, Nelson and Winnie paid their first visit to the United States. The man who had been a prisoner only five months earlier was

Nelson Mandela was given the key to New York City, where a huge parade was held in his honor. He was greeted by David Dinkins (left), the mayor of New York City, and by Mario Cuomo (right), the governor of New York State.

now treated like a king. His first stop was New York City, where more than 750,000 people gathered to watch a huge parade in his honor. The mayor of New York, a black man named David Dinkins, gave him the key to the city.

The next day, he visited a church, where 3,000 people came to see him. A South African celebration dance was performed, and the crowd was delighted to see Nelson join in. That night, 100,000 people came to hear him speak in Harlem, a mostly black section of New York City.

Nelson next went to a celebration in his honor at Yankee Stadium, where the New York Yankees play baseball. Nelson put on a baseball cap and joked to the audience, "I am a Yankee!" He was also invited to speak at the United Nations, or UN. The UN is located in New York City, and many nations belong to it. Its purpose is to allow governments to sit down and talk about their problems, so they can work out peaceful solutions.

Nelson's visit was not just a celebration though. At the United Nations, and just about everywhere else he spoke, he explained that the black people of South Africa need help from the rest of the world. He insisted that the United States and other countries continue to keep their money out of South Africa, to convince the government there that blacks must be given full freedom. Nelson also convinced Americans to donate a large amount of money to the African National Congress. Many times during their visit, he or Winnie would shout *Amandla!* to a crowd of people. The audience would answer them with *Ngawethu!* Together, they were saying "Power to the people!" These were the very same words that Nelson and his people had shouted to each other 27 years earlier, when he was being taken from a courtroom to prison.

During his trip, Nelson visited a total of eight U.S. cities, including Washington, D.C. He met with President George Bush, and the two men talked about what America could do to help change Nelson's country for the better.

Today black South Africans are still not free. There are some white South Africans who believe that the black citizens deserve equal rights, but there are far more who never want blacks to have total equality. To make matters worse, black South Africans have had trouble deciding which black leaders to follow. Many wish to be led by

Speaking at the United Nations, Nelson Mandela warned that black South Africans will need the world's help to win equal rights.

Nelson Mandela and the ANC, but some blacks want other leaders instead. This has led to fighting between black South Africans, something which has saddened the rest of the world.

In some ways, however, the chances for peace and freedom in South Africa seem better than ever. In 1990 the government began to allow blacks and whites to share certain areas, such as public parks and beaches. Also, President de Klerk and his government now want to talk with black leaders such as Nelson Mandela so that together they can solve the many problems faced by blacks and whites alike. In exchange, the ANC has agreed to stop violent protests, at least for now. Nelson and his followers want to see if equal rights can be won in a peaceful way. Meanwhile, if South Africans wish to see a day when all of its citizens are united, they need only stand on the shoulders of the thousands of blacks who have fought for freedom, and look into the future.

Chronology

July 18, 1918	Nelson Mandela born near Umtata, South Africa
1930	Mandela's father dies
1941	Mandela studies law in Johannesburg
1943	Joins the African National Congress (ANC)
June 14, 1958	Marries Winnie Madikizela
1961–62	Goes into hiding
Aug. 5, 1962	Arrested by South African police
June 11, 1964	Sentenced to life imprisonment on Robben Island
May 12, 1969	Winnie Mandela arrested and imprisoned, without trial, for 17 months

June 16, 1976	Soweto uprising begins
Dec. 23, 1977	Winnie Mandela forced to move to Brandfort
1978	P. W. Botha becomes president of South Africa
April 1982	Nelson Mandela transferred to Pollsmoor Prison
May 1984	Nelson and Winnie Mandela, for the first time in more than 20 years, are allowed to see each other without having a glass wall between them
1984–86	Mass revolts against apartheid occur throughout South Africa
Feb. 10, 1985	Nelson Mandela rejects conditional release offered by President Botha
1989	F. W. de Klerk becomes president of South Africa
Feb. 11, 1990	Nelson Mandela released from prison
June 1990	Nelson and Winnie Mandela visit the United States; Nelson Mandela meets with President Bush

Glossary

African National Congress   ANC; a group of black South Africans seeking to abolish apartheid

Afrikaner   a white South African descended from Dutch settlers

Amandla ngawethu   phrase meaning "power to the people"

apartheid   Dutch-based Afrikaner word meaning "apartness"; refers to the set of laws in South Africa that keep blacks and whites as separate as possible

civil war   a war that takes place between opposing groups of citizens within a country

continent   one of the seven divisions of land on earth (Africa, Antarctica, Asia, Australia, Europe, North America, and South America)

embassy the offices of representatives of a foreign country

homelands in South Africa, pieces of land reserved for blacks by the government

hunger strike an action in which people refuse to eat as a protest against a policy or action

protest a public expression of disapproval

quarry a pit from which building stone is removed

strike a group action in which people refuse to work as a protest against a policy or action

tribe a society united by kinship, culture, and language

United Nations UN; a worldwide organization of independent nations founded in 1945, after World War II, to promote international peace and cooperation

Zulu a South African tribe conquered by the Afrikaners

Picture Credits

Brian Feinberg, an editor and author, lives in New York City. Prior to entering book publishing he spent more than five years as a reporter for the *Commercial Appeal,* a daily newspaper in Memphis, Tennessee, and worked as an associate health editor for *Redbook* magazine.